BEYONCÉ

AND

JAY-Z

BEYONCÉ
AND
JAY-Z

Jacqueline Parrish

Rosen
YA™
New York

Published in 2020 by The Rosen Publishing Group, Inc.
29 East 21st Street, New York, NY 10010

Library of Congress Cataloging-in-Publication Data

Names: Parrish, Jacqueline, author. Title: Beyoncé and Jay–Z / Jacqueline Parrish.
Description: New York: Rosen Publishing, 2020 | Series: Power couples | Includes bibliographical references and index.
Identifiers: LCCN 2018048155| ISBN 9781508188797 (library bound) | ISBN 9781508188780 (pbk.)
Subjects: LCSH: Beyoncé, 1981– —Juvenile literature. | Jay-Z, 1969– —Juvenile literature. | Singers—United States—Biography—Juvenile literature. | Rap musicians—United States—Biography—Juvenile literature.
Classification: LCC ML3929 .P39 2019 | DDC 782.42164092/2 [B]—dc23
LC record available at ht tps://lccn.loc.gov/2018048155

Manufactured in China

On the cover: On July 18, 2014, Beyoncé and Jay-Z perform during the On the Run Tour at Minute Maid Park in Houston, Texas.

CONTENTS

INTRODUCTION

Beyoncé and Jay-Z are two renowned stars who have been in the limelight for more than a decade. Both are self-made individuals who climbed the ladder of success all the way to the top: Beyoncé, beginning as a young girl with a dream in Houston, Texas, and Jay-Z rising from the Marcy Houses projects in Brooklyn, New York. The power couple—two individuals who each have ambitious careers and who also work together to make their partnership equal and successful—is worth an estimated $1.25 billion, according to *Forbes* in July 2018, and live a lavish lifestyle with their three children. Beyoncé and Jay-Z have earned their money through musical performances, world tours, and album sales and both are accredited as music producers. Beyoncé's Formation World Tour alone brought in a quarter of a billion dollars, and their joint world tour, On the Run II, grossed $5 million each night, according to Hillary Hoffower for Business Insider.

Beyoncé and Jay-Z are business savvy. According to *Forbes* in March 2018, Jay-Z's fortune of $900 million comes mostly from Roc Nation, an entertainment company that he owns, as well as his large stake in the music-streaming company TIDAL and his interest in the expensive champagne

Beyoncé and Jay-Z perform in front of fans during their 2018 On the Run II Tour. Beyoncé announced on Instagram on March 12, 2018, that the iconic duo would tour once again.

Armand de Brignac. When Beyoncé isn't touring and making music, she is promoting her gym-wear line, Ivy Park, and her vegan meal on-demand delivery service, 22 Days Nutrition, which she created with her trainer Marco Borges. In addition, she has an endorsement with Pepsi that dates back to 2002. It was reported that she negotiated and signed a new multiyear endorsement deal with Pepsi in 2012 for an estimated $50 million, according to an article on *E! News* in September 2018.

The Carters both started their careers with a dream and determination for success. From Beyoncé's Houston, Texas, middle-class upbringing and membership in Girl's Tyme (the group that became Destiny's Child) to Jay-Z's early life in a poor neighborhood in Brooklyn, New York, rapping on street corners, these two have proved that you can do anything you want if you set your mind to it. Their talent, persistence, and drive have afforded them a life of luxury.

Jay-Z has thirteen albums, twenty-one Grammy Awards, and seventy-five Grammy nominations as of December 2018. He is tied with rapper Kanye West for rapper with the most Grammy wins, according to Grammy.com. He has also topped the *Billboard* 200 chart with fourteen number-one albums and is in second place for most chart-topping albums. The Beatles still hold the number-one spot with nineteen albums, according to Keith Caulfield for *Billboard*. Jay-Z has sold more than 36.3 million albums in the United States.

Beyoncé has seven hit albums, twenty-two Grammy Awards, and sixty-four Grammy nominations, as of December 2018. She is the most nominated female artist in history, according to Grammy.com. An August 29, 2016, article for *Billboard* reported that Beyoncé was the artist with the most Video Music Awards (VMAs), surpassing Madonna. Beyoncé is worth $350 million and has sold more than seventeen million albums in the United States.

The Carters own multimillion-dollar homes in Bel Air, a neighborhood of Los Angeles, California, and the Hamptons, in eastern Long Island in New York. They cruise around the Mediterranean Sea on a luxury yacht and travel the world, staying at the most magnificent destinations. They have become music industry royalty and they show no signs of giving up their thrones. This resource will chronicle their lives from big dreams as young children, their rise to the top, and how they became one of the most successful and influential power couples in the world.

CHAPTER 1

BECOMING QUEEN BEY

Beyoncé Giselle Knowles-Carter was born in Houston, Texas, on September 4, 1981, to Mathew and Tina Knowles. She grew up in an upper-middle-class family, her father, Mathew, was a successful salesman at Xerox Corporation, and Tina, her mother, owned a beauty salon called Headliners Hair Salon. Beyoncé has a younger sister, Solange, who was born in 1986. A few years after Beyoncé's birth, the Knowleses purchased a home in an upper-middle-class neighborhood in Houston's Third Ward. From an early age, Beyoncé liked to perform. When she was six years old, she

This aerial view of downtown Houston, Texas, includes the Third Ward, in the foreground of the photograph, where Beyoncé spent her childhood.

came home from school and belted out a nursery rhyme to her mother. Her mother was extremely impressed by how well Beyoncé could sing. Beyoncé could not only sing, but she could also act—she incorporated acting into the song. Beyoncé was a natural performer. According to the unauthorized biography *Becoming Beyoncé*, written by J. Randy Taraborrelli, Tina Knowles said, "I sat there thinking, 'My goodness, this is really … something.' It was a moment I don't think I'll ever forget."

GIRL'S TYME

Mathew Knowles saw how talented his daughter was and decided to dedicate himself to making her a star. He started a singing group called Girl's Tyme with Beyoncé and five other girls. In 1992, they secured a spot on a popular television talent program called *Star Search*. The Girl's Tyme crew—Beyoncé, LaTavia Roberson, Nina Taylor, Nicki Taylor, Kelly Rowland, and Ashley Davis—headed to Orlando, Florida, to tape their appearance on *Star Search* in November. This performance was key to their success; if they won they would secure a record deal, but if they lost they would be just another group that failed on *Star Search*.

Girl's Tyme decided to sing "That's the Way It Is in My City," with Beyoncé taking lead vocals. The girls waited for their announcement from Ed McMahon, the host of *Star Search*, on the darkened stage. Being on television for the first time made Beyoncé nervous. She had a lot of pressure on her to succeed because she took the lead in the performance. On stage, McMahon spoke into the microphone, "Welcome Beyoncé, LaTavia, Nina, Nicki, Kelly, and Ashley, the hip-hop, rapping Girl's Tyme." The girls had their cue to enter the stage as the lights went up and LaTavia was the first to perform. She started with a brief rap intro and then it was time for Beyoncé to take over. Beyoncé, being a natural entertainer, stole the spotlight, singing and dancing her way all over the

Ed McMahon, the host of *Star Search*, introduced Girl's Tyme during the group's 1992 appearance on the show.

stage. She, along with the rest of the girls, performed the best they could, but in the end they lost to a rock group called Skeleton Crew. Girl's Tyme received three out of five stars. Beyoncé forced a smile as the judges gave the group the bad news, but as soon as she walked off stage she cried.

DESTINY'S CHILD

Beyoncé's father quit his job to become Beyoncé's manager and focus on a new girl group, Destiny's Child. The new foursome consisted of Beyoncé, Kelly Rowland, LaTavia Roberson, and LeToya Luckett. Rowland had been a long-time friend of Beyoncé and her family, Roberson had auditioned for Girl's Tyme in 1990 and was a part of the girl group before the formation of Destiny's Child, and Luckett was a classmate of Beyoncé and joined the group after the departure of Ashley Davis in 1993. Three of the former Girl's Tyme members, Ashley Davis, Nicki Taylor, and Nina Taylor were no longer part of the group.

When Mathew quit his job, it put a lot of financial strain on the family. The Knowleses ended up selling their house and moving into a small apartment while Mathew managed Destiny's Child. Tina helped by making the girls' costumes and doing their hair. Tina devoted a lot of her time to making her salon a bigger success since they had one less paycheck coming in, and the girls would often come into the shop and sing for the women getting their hair styled.

THE BIG BREAK

In 1997, after many years of hard work and dedication, Destiny's Child signed a record contract with Columbia Records. Beyoncé would spend countless hours working on her songs, and she wasn't going

> We turned the volume up as loud as it could go and started running around the car singing along."
>
> —BEYONCÉ

to stop until she fulfilled her dream of becoming a professional singer. Her hard work paid off in 1998 when Destiny's Child released their first single, entitled "No, No, No," off the new album, *Destiny's Child*. The song was an instant hit and the album went to number four on the Billboard 200 pop chart where it stayed for twenty-six weeks. Beyoncé was on her way to becoming a bona fide celebrity, and she was only sixteen years old. She later recalled that the first time she heard the hit on the radio she was on her way to pick up her younger sister, Solange, from school. According to Taraborrelli in *Becoming Beyoncé*, Beyoncé said, "We turned the volume up as loud as it could go and started running around the car singing along." Destiny's Child sold more than one million copies and it was certified platinum, according to Billy Nilles on *E! News*.

The original members of Destiny's Child pose for a picture during the twelfth annual Soul Train Awards in 1998. *From left to right*: Kelly Rowland, Beyoncé Knowles, LeToya Luckett, and LaTavia Roberson.

In July 1999, Destiny's Child released their second album, *The Writing's on the Wall*. The songs "Say My Name" and "Bills, Bills, Bills" soared to number one on Billboard's Hot 100 singles chart. "Say My Name" won Destiny's Child their first Grammy Award, Best Rhythm and Blues (R&B) Performance by a Duo or Group with Vocals. Beyoncé started to let her creative juices flow and was credited as a writer of many of Destiny's Child's songs.

JEALOUSY FUELS A SPLIT

In 2000, LaTavia Roberson and LeToya Luckett sued Mathew Knowles for unfair treatment during their time in Destiny's Child, citing that he made Beyoncé the most important member of the group. The two women quit the group after their initial success and Beyoncé was heartbroken at their departure, according to Taraborrelli. Beyoncé believed that Destiny's Child was a family and watching two members walk away devastated her. For a month, she barely left her room, but her father, once again, came to the rescue with two new members for the girl group. Farrah Franklin and Michelle Williams would replace Roberson and Luckett to continue Destiny's Child's success. In the end, Roberson and Luckett reportedly ended up settling with a cash payout of $850,000. In 2002, the two would

(continued on the next page)

(continued from the previous page)

once again file a lawsuit against Beyoncé stating that the song "Survivor" was written about them. Beyoncé and the attorney for Destiny's Child, Tom Fulkerson, thought the lawsuit was ridiculous, according to a 2002 article in *Billboard*. The case was settled out of court for an undisclosed amount of money.

In 2000, LaTavia Roberson and LeToya Luckett filed a lawsuit against Beyoncé's father, over managerial and financial disagreements, and quit the group. Destiny's Child continued as a foursome with the introduction of Michelle Williams and Farrah Franklin in 2000, according to *Superstars of Hip-Hop: Beyoncé*, by Z. B. Hill. They started rehearsing immediately and performed at concerts as if the two original members had never left. The pressure of success and fame was too much for Farrah Franklin, unfortunately, and she quit Destiny's Child after a few months. The group decided not to replace Franklin, and it continued as a threesome. Losing another member of the group was unfortunate, but it fueled Beyoncé's desire to reach the top, so she pushed forward.

In 2001, Destiny's Child released their third album, *Survivor,* which soared to number one on the Billboard charts. *Survivor* was the first album with the group as a threesome, and it proved to be the most successful Destiny's Child album. According to Z. B. Hill, the album sold more than nine million copies worldwide and earned the group three Grammy nominations and a Grammy for Best R&B Performance by a Duo or Group with Vocals. *Survivor* was a pivotal album in Beyoncé's career, setting her apart from the other young women in the group because she wrote most of the album's songs and her vocals were so strong. Not only did she have a beautiful voice, but she was also a talented songwriter. She wrote "Bootylicious" about being happy with your body no matter what size you are. The same year the album was released, Beyoncé won an award for Songwriter of the Year. Beyoncé was the first African American woman to win this accolade.

GOING SOLO

After the success of *Survivor*, Destiny's Child decided to take a break and start their own solo careers. Beyoncé knew this step would be her time to shine all on her own. She was asked to play the character Foxxy Cleopatra in the comedy movie *Austin Powers in Goldmember* in 2001. Beyoncé, a natural singer and performer, had a hard time acting. A rumor spread on set that Beyoncé was holding up production because she couldn't remember her lines. Beyoncé persevered and the movie was released in the summer of 2002 to mixed reviews.

Beyoncé (*second from left*), her father, Mathew (*far left*), mother, Tina (*far right*), and sister, Solange (*third from left*), attend the premiere of *Austin Powers in Goldmember* in 2002.

TO INFINITY AND BEYONCÉ

Beyoncé released her first solo album, *Dangerously in Love,* in 2003. The single "Crazy in Love," featured veteran rapper Jay-Z and both the album and the single shot to number one on Billboard's charts. According to *Billboard*, the album sold more than five million copies in the United States and won the Grammy for Best Contemporary R&B album. "Crazy in Love" won the Grammy for Best R&B Song and Best Rap/Song Collaboration. The album

ENTER JAY-Z

By the time Beyoncé started collaborating with Jay-Z in 2002, he had already released seven hit albums and was worth an estimated $120 million, according to Taraborrelli. He has been called the greatest rapper alive and he caught the young star's eye. Beyoncé and Jay-Z were very different people when they met. Beyoncé was just beginning her career and was more into the victory of her success than the money. Jay-Z was into designer clothes and jewelry, and money meant success to the hip-hop star. They collaborated on a couple of songs: "03 Bonnie and Clyde" and "Crazy in Love."

turned Beyoncé into a worldwide sensation. "Crazy in Love" is listed as one of the greatest songs of the century by the magazine *Rolling Stone*. The young girl from Houston, with big dreams of becoming a professional singer, was an international success.

Beyoncé released her second solo album, *B'Day*, on September 4, 2006. The song "Irreplaceable" hit number one on the *Billboard* Hot 100 chart. The song also became the bestselling US single of 2007, and the album sold more than eight million copies worldwide. While Beyoncé was enjoying her success as a solo music artist, she also took on more acting roles, as Xania in *The Pink Panther* (2006) and as

Deena Jones in *Dreamgirls* (2006). Beyoncé was now a celebrity. She posed on the cover of magazines, sold millions of albums globally, and dabbled in acting. She was on the fast track to the top.

In 2008, Beyoncé released her fourth solo album, *I Am … Sasha Fierce.* Sasha Fierce was Beyoncé's alter ego from her childhood. To help her feel more confident while she was performing she would pretend her name was Sasha, and Sasha had a last name, Fierce. Beyoncé was two people, a typical young woman from Houston, Texas, and another whom she adapted as her stage presence. The single "Single Ladies (Put a Ring on It)" would change the track of Beyoncé's already successful career by introducing the theme of female empowerment. It promoted the idea of ditching a dead-end relationship and Beyoncé made it feel cool and powerful. The song was one of Beyoncé's most successful of her career. According to Lacey Rose for *Forbes*, the song was number one on Billboard's Hot 100 and the album would end up selling more than four million copies worldwide. At the 2009 Grammy Awards, Beyoncé took home six Grammys, including Song of the Year with "Single Ladies (Put a Ring on It)." The win would set a record for the most Grammys won by a female artist at one award show.

CHAPTER 2

HARD KNOCK LIFE: JAY-Z'S RAGS TO GLOBAL DOMINATION

Shawn Corey Carter, better known by his stage name Jay-Z, was born on December 4, 1969, in Brooklyn, New York. Jay-Z was the youngest of four children born to Gloria Carter and Adnis Reeves. He had two older sisters, Andrea, called Annie, and Michelle, called Mickey, and an older brother, Eric. He grew up in the Marcy Houses, a rough housing project full of crime, in Brooklyn. It was common for the young Jay-Z to witness drug deals in the corridors of Marcy's halls and police raids looking for guns, drugs, and wanted gang members. The elevated

The Marcy Houses in Brooklyn, New York, are pictured here. Jay-Z lived in the Marcy Houses as a child. He has mentioned them in many of his rap songs.

tracks of the J and Z subway lines run a few blocks from the Marcy Houses, which might have contributed to his stage name.

Jay-Z's parents had a huge vinyl record collection. At night when the children were in bed, they would often play music and Jay-Z would sneak to the door in his pajamas to watch his parents and their friends and listen and dance to the music. From an early age, Jay-Z had a love of music. He would walk the streets and listen to the city sounds and rap on street corners about his life experiences. His incessant drumming on the kitchen table led his mother to buy him a boom box. His friends called him Jazzy.

Jay-Z was a smart kid and played Little League baseball. His older brother, Eric, would go on to play college basketball, so athletic ability ran in the family. He had a photographic memory and excelled in his studies at a young age. He lost interest in school the older he got and spent more time on the streets. His father, Adnis, took Jay-Z on trips to Manhattan to visit Times Square. Young Jay and his father would watch people in Times Square, and Adnis would quiz Jay on what size clothing he thought the people were wearing. After trips to the city, Adnis would make Jay-Z lead the way back to the subway station to learn leadership skills and how to take responsibility. Jay-Z and his father shared a close bond.

FAMILY TURMOIL

When Jay-Z was eleven years old, his father abandoned his family. The departure of his father had a big impact on Jay-Z. In Mark Beaumont's book *Jay Z: The King of America* (2012), Jay-Z is quoted as saying, "Once you've let yourself fall that in love with someone, once you put him on such a high pedestal and he lets you down, you never want to experience that pain again. So I just remember being really quiet and really cold." The aftermath of his father's abandonment turned Jay-Z onto rap and it became an outlet for him and his feelings.

At the age of twelve, Jay-Z's life changed when he accidentally shot his brother, Eric, in the arm after he caught Eric trying to steal from him to support his drug addiction. Eric didn't press charges against Jay-Z because Eric knew what he did was wrong. He should have never tried to steal from a family member. Jay-Z didn't mean to shoot his brother; he just wanted to scare him. Ultimately, Eric forgave Jay-Z. People close to Jay saw this shooting incident as the start of his downward spiral into selling drugs and thinking he was above the law. In *Jay-Z: The King of America*, Beaumont writes:

> He'd never meant to shoot Eric, himself just four years older than Shawn. He'd got the gun from a friend's place (it was easy enough to find—guns were everywhere in the projects)

just to wave in his face, scare him enough that he'd stop stealing his own family's possessions to feed his crack habit.

The incident shook up the young Jay-Z, and he was glad that his brother forgave him.

While Jay-Z was still a teenager, he began selling drugs to earn money. The hustling game seemed to be the right path to take because in the projects drugs were rampant. The potential to escape the projects and find lucrative work was slim to none and a lot of young teens turned to crime for money. During a drug deal gone bad, he almost lost his life and credited his survival to a divine intervention when the person shooting didn't really know how to shoot a gun. Jay-Z decided he wanted to pursue music and leave the life of hustling drugs behind him. It would prove to be the best decision he ever made and started him on the fast track to a prosperous career.

INTRODUCING JAY-Z

Jay-Z, along with friends Damon Dash and Kareem Burke, started an independent record label they called Roc-A-Fella Records in 1995. On this label, he released *Reasonable Doubt*, his first album in 1996. Jay-Z realized that hip-hop was his true calling in life, and he was proud that he had escaped the criminal life in the projects. *Reasonable Doubt* had

Jay-Z accepts the award for Best Rap Video during the 1999 MTV Video Music Awards.

a few tracks that were semiautobiographical, about Jay-Z and his life on the streets.

In November 1997, Jay-Z released his second album, *In My Lifetime ... Vol. 1*. The album, which talked about his childhood and criminal past, earned him a spot at number three on the *Billboard* Top 200. Although this album was more successful than *Reasonable Doubt*, it established Jay-Z's name in the rap world in the post Biggie Smalls and Tupac era. After the death of Biggie Smalls in 1997, the position was open for a new rap kingpin on the East Coast and Jay-Z saw this vacuum as an opportunity to claim the title.

In 1998, Jay-Z released *Vol. 2 ... Hard Knock Life,* and the album sold more than five million copies, according to *Complex* magazine in 2018, and earned him the Grammy for Best Rap Album. The album went to number one on the *Billboard* Top 200. The song "Hard Knock Life" became an instant hit and is still one of his best-selling singles to date. The album catalyzed his career, making him one of the most influential and successful hip-hop artists.

In 1999, Jay-Z released *Vol. 3 ... Life and Times of S. Carter.* A few months prior to the release of the album, he had been featured on Mariah Carey's hit "Heartbreaker." It softened his image as a hardcore rapper because he collaborated on a pop song with one of the hottest pop acts of the time. The song rose to number one on *Billboard*'s Hot 100 Singles chart and boosted his reputation as a multidimensional

JAY-Z'S LEGAL TROUBLE

Jay-Z was excited to release *Vol 3 ... Life and Times of S. Carter* after the triumph of his previous album, *Vol 2 ... Hard Knock Life*. There was word on the street that the album was already being bootlegged and Jay-Z was furious. Lance Rivera, a producer for Def Jam Records, was the person everyone was pointing a finger at. Jay-Z confronted Rivera at the Kit Kat Club in 1999, and the incident ended with Jay-Z stabbing Rivera in the stomach. The injuries were not life threatening, but Jay-Z was facing up to seventeen years in prison if convicted by a grand jury. Jay-Z knew he had to be more careful with his temper in the future. Jay-Z pleaded guilty to third-degree assault and was put on probation for three years.

act. Jay-Z's career was soaring to new heights, and he was enjoying the fame and the money. According to *Jay-Z: The King of America,* the album *Vol. 3... Life and Times of S. Carter* became *Billboard*'s first number-one album of the new millennium.

In 2001, Jay-Z released *Blueprint,* an album that would solidify him as one of the greatest rappers and powerful voices going into the twenty-first century. The album rose to number one on *Billboard*'s Top R&B/ Hip-Hop Albums chart. *Blueprint* is listed as number

Jay-Z performs at a 9/11 benefit concert at Madison Square Garden in New York City in 2001. The concert's proceeds went to the New York Police & Fire Widows' & Children's Benefit Fund.

252 on *Rolling Stone* magazine's 500 Greatest Albums of All Time. According to *Jay-Z: A Biography of a Hip-Hop Icon,* the album sold more than half a million copies in the first week of its release.

JAY-Z MEETS BEYONCÉ

In the fall of 2002, Jay-Z approached Beyoncé about collaborating on a song with him. The song was "'03 Bonnie and Clyde." The two knew each other through the celebrity scene but had never worked together. Beyoncé, raised in an upper-middle-class family and a devout Methodist, and Jay-Z, who had grown up peddling crack on the streets of Brooklyn and was still on probation for assault when he met the young diva, seemed an unlikely pair. The likelihood of a relationship between the two seemed to be slim to none. The song, however, was successful, and rose to number four on the US *Billboard* chart. They also collaborated on "Crazy in Love," a single off Beyoncé's first solo album, *Dangerously in Love,* in 2003.

Beyoncé and Jay-Z began dating a few months after their collaboration on "'03 Bonnie and Clyde." The couple kept their relationship private even when photos were published of them embracing each other. Beyoncé shrugged it off, stating that the two were just good friends and she wasn't dating anyone in particular. According to an April 5, 2005, article in *People* magazine, during a 2002 taping of *TRL* on MTV, Jay-Z said of Beyoncé, "She's a lovely girl. We're getting to know each other." Beyoncé and

THE SECRET SON

In 2016, Rymir Satterthwaite publicly claimed he was Jay-Z's son. The twenty-four-year-old aspiring rapper said that his mother, Wanda, had had a relationship with Jay-Z in 1992, according to *Complex*, when she was sixteen years old. Rymir and his mother tried contacting Jay-Z in 2009 for a paternity test, but the rapper had avoided the request. On his new album *Everything Is Love*, the song "Heard About Us" addresses the rumor, comparing it to "Billie Jean," a well-known song from pop icon Michael Jackson about a denial of paternity. Jay-Z has not spoken publicly about the paternity case.

Jay-Z are extremely private about their personal lives. According to the book *Superstars of Hip-Hop: Beyoncé,* Beyoncé said about her love life, "I'll tell my friends. I just don't feel comfortable telling the whole world."

RETIREMENT AND BUSINESS VENTURES

In 2003, Jay-Z announced his retirement from performing as a rapper before he released his latest album, *The Black Album*. The song "99 Problems" won Jay-Z another Grammy for Best Rap Solo Performance. Jay-Z's farewell concert was held at Madison Square

Garden in New York City on November 25, 2003. The management staff at Madison Square Garden were concerned because hip-hop concerts had the reputation of bringing unnecessary violence, and they had not had a hip-hop artist perform in many years. The tickets sold out the twenty-thousand-seat arena in five minutes. Jay-Z had risen far from his days in the Marcy Houses, selling drugs, and rapping on street corners. He was now selling out one of the biggest arenas in the world.

> "I have taken the whole ride. I didn't skip any floors. I started at the lower lobby. I went all the way up to the penthouse."
>
> —JAY-Z

In 2004, Jay-Z turned his attention to business ventures but continued to collaborate on songs with various artists, such as Linkin Park, Alicia Keys, Beyoncé, and Rihanna. He was the president and chief executive officer (CEO) of Def Jam Records from 2004 to 2008, had a lucrative clothing line called Roca Wear, was a part owner of the 40/40 Club, a nightclub in New York City, had a contract with Reebok and was the only nonathlete to acquire his own shoe, and was part owner of the New Jersey Nets, a National Basketball Association (NBA) team. There was a conflict of interest between Damon Dash and Jay-Z, which ultimately ended with Jay-Z backing out of Roc-A-Fella Records and becoming CEO of Def Jam Records. Def Jam would end up buying Roc-A-Fella in 2004. According to the book *Jay-Z:*

Jay-Z holds up a New Jersey Nets basketball jersey. Jay-Z was part owner of the NBA team and was influential in relocating the team to Brooklyn, New York.

Building a Hip-Hop Empire, Jay-Z said, "I have taken the whole ride. I didn't skip any floors. I started at the lower lobby. I went all the way up to the penthouse."

Jay-Z has proven to be a successful hip-hop artist as well as a smart businessman. As of July 2017, he has sold more than thirty-six million albums in the United States alone, according to *Jay-Z: Building a Hip-Hop Empire,* and has received a multitude of Grammy nominations and awards to boot. Jay-Z, a self-made rapper from the streets of Brooklyn, has worked very hard to forge a legacy as a billionaire rap mogul and Renaissance man.

CHAPTER 3

THE RISE OF A POWER COUPLE

On April 4, 2008, Beyoncé and Jay-Z were married in New York City. The wedding took place in Jay-Z's seventh-floor loft and welcomed forty guests. The wedding was small and intimate despite the level of fame the two shared. The guests were asked to leave their cell phones with the drivers who drove them to the wedding. It was not professionally catered; instead, Beyoncé's mom, Tina, and Jay-Z's grandmother, Hattie, prepared the meal. Despite being a powerhouse brand, the couple managed to keep the wedding private and small. In September

Beyoncé flashes her $5 million dollar, eighteen-carat flawless diamond engagement ring, designed by acclaimed jeweler Lorraine Schwartz.

2008, Beyoncé finally showcased her $5 million wedding ring. According to the book *Empire State of Mind: How Jay Z Went From Street Corner to Corner Office*, music historian Jeff Chang said, "It's two superpowers coming together. It's sort of Microsoft and Apple deciding they can be literally in bed together." The two, being successful independently, merged into a marriage combining their fame and fortune and becoming a powerhouse celebrity couple.

JAY-Z AND ROC NATION

In 2008, Roc Nation was born. Founded by Jay-Z, Roc Nation is an American entertainment company that caters to professional athletes, musicians, producers, and songwriters. Their initiative is to promote celebrities through artist management, production, and touring. A list of notable clients for Roc Nation includes Big Sean, Rihanna, and Shakira. In 2013, Jay-Z founded Roc Nation Sports to work in the same way with athletes that they do with musicians. They step in and help the athlete with endorsement deals, media relations, and community outreach. Roc Nation Sports works with big names, including football player Dez Bryant, baseball player Robinson Canó, and basketball player Kevin Durant, among others. On the Roc Nation website, it states:

> Since its founding in 2008, Roc Nation has grown into the world's preeminent entertainment

Professional basketball player Kevin Durant attends a Roc Nation Sports party at the 40/40 Club. Durant is represented by Jay-Z's company Roc Nation Sports.

company. We've forged strong partnerships with the world's leading experts in artist management, technology, fashion, and philanthropy, and are redefining the business of entertainment.

On October 4, 2018, *Variety* magazine reported that Roc Nation was teaming up with the BBC for a TV adaptation of Noughts and Crosses, a young adult novel series written by Malorie Blackman. Roc Nation will executive produce the series and provide the soundtrack. Noughts and Crosses is a series that takes place in an alternate society where white people, members of the underclass, are discriminated against and black people are the ruling class. The series relates the love story between a young couple, a cross and a nought, in a world of segregation and prejudice.

4, MTV MUSIC AWARDS, AND BLUE IVY

In 2011, Beyoncé released her fourth solo album, *4*, and like her previous albums before, it debuted at number one on the charts. She executive produced the album and also cowrote the majority of the songs. Babyface, a producer, songwriter, and singer, wrote the song "Best Thing I Never Had" on the album and said it was a dream come true working with Beyoncé. In a 2011 review by Erika Ramirez for *Billboard*, Babyface said, "What is the definition of perfection ... or the closest thing to it? Beyoncé. Icons are made. Stars are

> I put a lot of thought into how I wanted to unveil it. It was important to me that I was able to do it myself. I was extremely nervous. It was the toughest red carpet I ever did."
>
> —BEYONCÉ

born. From the moment Beyoncé took her first breath, her star was shining. What an honor it is for me to say that I danced with a true star, or wrote."

In August 2011, Beyoncé performed "Love on Top" at the MTV Music Awards and showcased a baby bump. She announced, "Tonight I want you to stand up on your feet, tonight I want you to feel the love that's growing inside of me." After the performance, she dropped the microphone, unbuttoned her blazer, and rubbed her stomach. In an interview with *Harper's Bazaar* on October 11, 2011, Beyoncé said she had carefully planned how she wanted to announce to the world her pregnancy news. "I put a lot of thought into how I wanted to unveil it. It was important to me that I was able to do it myself. I was extremely nervous. It was the toughest red carpet I ever did." This iconic moment broke the *Guinness World Records* record for "most tweets per second recorded for a single event" with 8,868 tweets per second.

During an interview on an Australian TV show called *Sunday Night*, Beyoncé sat down and it appeared that her stomach folded over. A lot of speculation swirled on the internet that she was faking her pregnancy and she had actually hired a surrogate because she didn't want to ruin her figure. People began to examine the

Beyoncé motions to her baby bump as she happily announces her pregnancy at the 2011 MTV Video Music Awards.

video and criticize that she didn't sit down the way a normal pregnant woman would. They also examined her "baby bump" to determine how big or small she was in comparison to her due date. The story became big news. All the major media outlets were reporting on the rumor that she was faking her pregnancy. According to *Becoming Beyoncé*, Beyoncé responded, "To think that I would be that vain. I respect mothers and women so much, and to be able to experience bringing a child into this world if you're lucky and fortunate enough to experience that. I would never ever take that for granted." Beyoncé was hurt by the accusations. Not many people knew that a couple of years before her pregnancy with Blue Ivy she had suffered a miscarriage.

Blue Ivy Carter was born on January 7, 2012, at Lenox Hill Hospital in New York City. Jay-Z and Beyoncé booked an entire wing of the hospital for the birth and even had windows blacked out on the maternity floor so people would not see them coming and going from the hospital room. The couple spent $1.3 million to rent the wing of the maternity ward, according to an article in the *Washington Post*. Their security team also asked hospital management to put black tape on the security cameras on her floor to ensure absolute privacy for the power pop singer. The Carters' security team also installed a bulletproof door to Beyoncé's maternity room. This secrecy only fueled speculation that Beyoncé was never pregnant.

Beyoncé steps out in public with her daughter, Blue Ivy, for the first time in 2012.

TROUBLE IN PARADISE?

Beyoncé released her fifth album, entitled *Beyoncé*, on July 15, 2014. She won Grammys for Best R&B Performance and Best R&B Song with "Drunk in Love," a song she collaborated with her husband on. Beyoncé and Jay-Z headlined a tour, On the Run, in 2014. It was the first time the power duo had headlined a tour together.

In 2016, Beyoncé released *Lemonade*, which further fueled speculation about Jay-Z's infidelity. Irrelevant to the adultery supposition, *Lemonade* showcased a new Beyoncé, a feminist Beyoncé. She bled her emotions into the songs, creating a different, more powerful, and raw style from that of her previous albums. The album was an opening into her emotions and her experiences as an African American woman. At the Fifty-Ninth Annual Grammy Awards, Beyoncé took home two Grammys, Best Urban Contemporary Album, and Best Music Video for "Formation." The 2016 Super Bowl halftime show displayed a Black Panther Party–themed performance by Beyoncé, mixing themes of female empowerment and social justice and creating a new, stronger image for the power pop singer.

In 2017, Jay-Z released his album, *4:44*, on TIDAL, a music-streaming service that he co-owns with other artists. The album is, in part, a response

THE ELEVATOR INCIDENT

In May 2014, Jay-Z, Beyoncé, and Solange attended the Met Gala, a fundraiser for New York City's Metropolitan Museum of Art's Costume Institute. Video surveillance in an elevator captured Solange, who is known to be very protective of her sister, throwing punches and kicking Jay-Z while Beyoncé remained a bystander. The video shows Beyoncé quietly stepping back so Solange can continue her assault on Jay-Z. Although no one knows exactly what prompted Solange to attack Jay-Z, there is speculation that Jay-Z wanted to attend an after-party hosted by Rihanna, a celebrity and singer with whom Jay-Z had supposedly had an affair. Rumors once again swirled about Jay-Z's infidelity in the marriage but also that it might have been an attention-getting move because it gave them a lot of it right before their tour. According to *Becoming Beyoncé*, Beyoncé's father, Mathew, suspected that the fight was staged to promote Beyoncé and Jay-Z's On the Run Tour.

to the so-called affair that he was accused of on Beyoncé's *Lemonade*, an album that was also released on TIDAL.

WEALTHIEST STARS IN HIP-HOP

In 2018, an article in *Forbes* named Jay-Z the wealthiest hip-hop artist of all time. Jay-Z has the mind of a businessman, and his stakes in TIDAL and Roc Nation have earned him the crown as the richest rapper alive. From 2017 to 2018, Jay-Z's net worth skyrocketed from $810 million to $900 million, according to *Forbes*. Another contributor to his success has been his interest in the $300-a-bottle champagne, Armand de Brignac. In 2017, Beyoncé and Jay-Z purchased a mansion in Los Angeles for $88 million. The power couple took out a $59-million mortgage and, according to an article in Business Insider in March 2018, the home purchase was the sixth priciest in the history of Los Angeles.

INTRODUCING TWINS

On February 1, 2017, Beyoncé announced on an Instagram post that she and Jay-Z were expecting twins. This post was another example of Beyoncé's controlling what she allows the public to know. The announcement stated, "We are incredibly grateful that our family will be growing by two." It was signed: The Carters. The Instagram announcement broke another record for *Guinness World Records* for the "most liked image on Instagram." The post had surpassed five million likes in as little as three hours. Queen Bey, once again, reigned supreme.

CHAPTER 4

THE EMPIRE STATE OF MIND: POWER COUPLE DYNAMICS

Beyoncé and Jay-Z might be known for their musical endeavors, but they also contribute their time and money to charitable causes. Like their relationship, many of their charitable donations are private but that doesn't mean they aren't reaching out and giving back. Their belief is that the world has given them a lot so they are going to give back to the world.

THE SHAWN CARTER FOUNDATION

In 2003, Jay-Z, with the help of his mother, Gloria Carter, established the Shawn Carter Foundation, which provided money for scholarships for disadvantaged

Jay-Z (*center*) headlines a benefit concert at Carnegie Hall for the Shawn Carter Foundation and the United Way of New York City in 2012.

youths. The foundation raises money for college scholarships, college-counseling programs, study-abroad opportunities, college visits, and personal development to name a few. Since the introduction of the Shawn Carter Foundation in 2003, it has successfully raised more than $4 million toward scholarship funds, according to Gail Mitchell for *Billboard*. The majority of the recipients have faced socioeconomic hardships, as well as teenage pregnancy and homelessness, that have made it harder for them to pursue a higher education. According to the Shawn

Carter Foundation website, 79 percent of scholarship holders were from single-parent households and 77 percent came from households with an annual income of under $40,000.

SURVIVOR FOUNDATION, PHOENIX HOUSE, AND BEYGOOD

In 2005, Beyoncé, with the help of Kelly Rowland, Mathew Knowles, Tina Knowles, and Solange Knowles, founded the Survivor Foundation, which assisted victims of Hurricane Katrina. During her 2006 tour, Beyoncé held food drives to help those displaced by the hurricane. The Survivor Foundation aided people who lost their homes during the catastrophic natural disaster by providing temporary housing during the transition period to a new home. In 2007, she also founded the Knowles-Temenos Place Apartments, a housing unit that helped people who had been displaced from their homes. According to Taylor Lewis of *Essence*, Beyoncé had donated more than $7 million as of 2016 to help keep the complex running.

In 2009, during the filming of *Cadillac Records*, Beyoncé was introduced to Phoenix House, a network of rehabilitation centers for drug addicts and alcoholics. In the movie, she played Etta James, a singer who lived a tumultuous life as an addict. She donated her $4 million salary from the film to Phoenix House and created a cosmetology school where recovering addicts can learn skills to use in everyday life.

BeyGood Foundation is an organization that helps make the world a better place. Created in 2013 during her Mrs. Carter Show World Tour, Beyoncé worked with local charities in the cities where she was performing to raise awareness for local causes. The BeyGood Foundation helps people who are homeless, sick, and unemployed. At her concerts, there would be tables set up where concertgoers could donate money to the charities she had picked. BeyGood Houston helped victims in the wake of Hurricane Harvey. The organization aimed to provide baby products, feminine products, cots, and blankets to help after the widespread destruction caused by the hurricane. Beyoncé was named as a top charitable celebrity in 2016 on DoSomething.org's list of charitable celebrities, and in 2017, she was named one of the most charitable celebrities, according to Rachel George for *Billboard*.

HURRICANE MARIA, PUERTO RICO, AND TIDAL

In 2017, after the devastation of Hurricane Maria, Jay-Z teamed up with fellow rapper Fat Joe and provided planes to send shipments of supplies to Puerto Rico to help the residents. Jay-Z also loaned out the 40/40 Club for an invitation-only charity event that raised more money for Puerto Rico in the aftermath of the hurricane. In an article in *Vibe*

Beyoncé walks the "Fashion for Relief" runway to raise money to aid Hurricane Katrina victims. She and other celebrities appeared at the closing of the Olympus Fashion Week Spring 2006 show.

magazine on October 4, 2017, it was said that all goods brought to the club for the fundraiser would be loaded on a plane and the supplies sent directly to Puerto Rico, "The invite for the 40/40 event, which is being organized by the Puerto Rican Family Institute and Big & Little Skills Academy, asks people to bring school supplies, flashlights, solar lamps and batteries. A plane will also reportedly be sending the supplies collected at the event on Thursday (Oct. 5)." Jay-Z's music-streaming company, TIDAL, sponsored a benefit concert and all of the ticket sales went directly to organizations that help with disaster relief. Other notable artists who performed that night were Stevie Wonder, Cardi B, and Jennifer Lopez.

THE PRINCE'S TRUST AND GLOBAL CITIZEN

In 2018, Beyoncé and Jay-Z offered fans free tickets to their On the Run II Tour if they donated to a charitable cause. The power couple partnered with two nonprofit organizations, The Prince's Trust and Global Citizen. The Prince's Trust helps disadvantaged youth, and Global Citizen is a movement designed to help end extreme poverty. The two organizations raffled concert tickets to people who donated to the cause or volunteered their time. On the *Good Morning America* website in June 2018, Nick Stace, the chief executive of the Prince's Trust in the United Kingdom said:

BAILOUTS

Jay-Z and Beyoncé wired tens of thousands of dollars to bail out protestors arrested during Black Lives Matter protests in Baltimore, Maryland, and Ferguson, Missouri, after civil unrest broke out in response to the deaths of Michael Brown and Freddie Gray, two men killed at the hands of police officers in those cities in 2015. The donations were kept quiet at the time, but it was confirmed that the couple had helped bail people out of jail, although the specifics remain uncertain. According to Dream Hampton, a writer and activist for Black Lives Matter, in an article for CBS News, she confirmed that the duo donated the money but that Beyoncé and Jay-Z "insist folk keep quiet" regarding the generosity. Beyoncé and Jay-Z attended the Rally 4 Peace concert held in May 2015 after the huge protest in Baltimore. Prince headlined the concert and released a song called "Baltimore" in the wake of the brutal death of Freddie Gray. TIDAL streamed the concert for free on its website. Any donations that were received through the TIDAL website were given to the Baltimore Justice Fund, which was created to provide awareness for racial injustice and police accountability.

Beyoncé has supported The Prince's Trust for many years and understands the importance of giving young people who have faced setbacks

Beyoncé and Jay-Z perform during their On the Run II Tour in 2018. The couple offered free tickets to fans who donated to a charitable cause.

in life the chance of a brighter future. We aim to empower them with the confidence and skills they need to take control of their lives and realize their ambitions, so that they can live, learn and earn.

For volunteering your time, there was a chance to win tickets to the concert and there was also an auction for a lucky fan to win VIP tickets.

FORMATION SCHOLARS

On the one-year anniversary of her hit album *Lemonade*, Beyoncé introduced a scholarship program for women called the Formation Scholars. The Formation Scholars awarded money to four women who were confident and creative and pursuing degrees in literature, music, African American studies, and creative arts. The women would receive $25,000 toward their education. To qualify for the Formation Scholarship, each woman wrote an essay on how *Lemonade* inspired her professionally and academically. The four colleges that participated in the program were Howard University, Parsons School of Design, Spelman College, and Berklee College of Music. The four women chosen for the award in 2017 were all academically successful, with a GPA of 3.5 or higher. The winners were Sadiya Ramos, Avery Youngsblood, Maya Rogers, and Bria Paige.

THE POWER OF BEY

The September 2018 issue of *Vogue* featured Beyoncé on the cover. The photographer she chose to photograph her was a twenty-three-year-old African American, Tyler Mitchell. It was the first time in *Vogue* history that an African American shot a cover photo for the magazine. In the interview published in that issue of *Vogue*, Beyoncé said, "It's important to me that I help open doors for younger artists. There are so many cultural and societal barriers to entry that I like to do what I can to level the playing field, to present a different point of view for people who may feel like their voices don't matter."

The September 2018 issue of *Vogue* was just a taste of the power and influence Beyoncé has. The popular magazine has been in circulation for 126 years and yet had never had an African American photograph the cover before. The iconic photo shoot will certainly help boost Mitchell's career because Beyoncé used her power to get him the job. Generally, the magazine's editors pick the photographer for the cover, not the person being featured. It is another example of Beyoncé taking charge and using her notoriety to change an unequal system.

"
It's important to me that I help open doors for younger artists. There are so many cultural and societal barriers to entry that I like to do what I can to level the playing field, to present a different point of view for people who may feel like their voices don't matter."

—BEYONCÉ

CHAPTER 5

BEYONCÉ AS A FEMINIST AND POP CULTURE ICON

Beyoncé and Jay-Z are no strangers to life in the public eye. Together they have accomplished artistic success, marriage, parenthood, and financial power. Beyoncé's *Lemonade* showcased a different side to the R&B diva. In the narrative movie *Lemonade*, Malcolm X, the civil rights activist and minister who introduced the concept of black racial pride, is heard saying, "The most disrespected person in America is the black woman. The most unprotected person in America is the black woman. The most neglected person in America is the black woman." The movie is about a black woman and starring a black woman and brings the struggles and triumphs of black women to the forefront of our culture. In her September 2018 *Vogue* interview, Beyoncé said, "When I first started,

BODY POSITIVE AND GIRL POWER

Beyoncé is no stranger to promoting a positive body image and female empowerment through her music. Songs such as "Bootylicious," "Check on It," "Run the World (Girls)," and "Survivor" are just a few of the songs that come to mind. "Run the World (Girls)" is a song about empowering yourself by any means necessary, an influential song about female empowerment that all women can enjoy. "Survivor" was a Destiny's Child hit about surviving any situation and coming out stronger on the other side. "Check on It" and "Bootylicious" are body-positive songs about loving your body and showing it off. In 2014, Beyoncé released a twelve-minute short film titled "Yours and Mine." In the film she said, "We do not value ourselves enough. Especially young people, [who] don't really appreciate, how brilliant our bodies are. I've always been very, very specific, and very choosy—*very* choosy—about what I do with my body, and who I want to share that with." She also went on to speak about happiness saying, "Happiness comes from you. No one else can make you happy. *You* make you happy."

21 years ago, I was told that it was hard for me to get onto covers of magazines because black people did not sell." Clearly she has proved that statement incorrect. Beyoncé has shattered the glass ceiling of the male-dominated music industry, embracing her femininity and sexuality and proving she can acquire fame and fortune. Beyoncé has branded herself a feminist and has become a strong role model for women, particularly African American women.

GIRL POWER

Beyoncé performed at the 2013 Super Bowl halftime show. She had a backup band of all women (The Sugar Mamas), women backup dancers, and women backup singers. In an article in *Ms.* magazine in March 2015, Aishah Shahidah Simmons, a documentary filmmaker and feminist writer said, "Her Super Bowl performance clearly turned the patriarchy on its head. Her inclusion of an all-woman band, owning her sexual power, her presentation of such a diverse group of women (African Americans, Latinas, Asians)—she was definitely in a place of power." The performance showcased complete female power; however, some people were quick to criticize. Many people said she needed to wear more clothes to

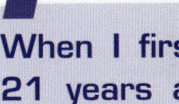

> When I first started, 21 years ago, I was told that it was hard for me to get onto covers of magazines because black people did not sell."
>
> —BEYONCÉ

In February 2013, Beyoncé (*center*) is reunited during the Super Bowl Halftime Show with Destiny's Child's Kelly Rowland (*left*) and Michelle Williams (*right*).

cover her body while performing and that her dance moves were too sexy, but Beyoncé brought power to her performance.

In an interview with *GQ* by Amy Wallace, entitled "Miss Millennium: Beyoncé," Beyoncé said, "I truly believe that women should be financially independent from their men. And let's face it, money gives men the power to run the show. It gives men the power to define value. They define what's sexy. And men define what's feminine. It's ridiculous." Beyoncé made a name for herself before she married Jay-Z and continues to dominate all on her own. Still, many critics debate whether Beyoncé is indeed a feminist. According to Janell Hobson in *Ms.* magazine, their argument is that she sings about female independence from men in "Bills, Bills, Bills" and "Single Ladies (Put a Ring on It)" but she also sings about pleasing men, in "Cater 2 U" and also in headlining a tour called "The Mrs. Carter Show World Tour." Simmons relates that Beyoncé is seen as antifeminist because of racial politics. She said, "If Beyoncé were white, she would definitely be called a feminist. But mainstream culture often doesn't recognize women of color in that way."

Beyoncé's *Lemonade* is not only a successful album but also a work of art. Numerous feminist scholars debate whether Beyoncé is a feminist or not. The album represents black womanhood as a strong band of sisters who will not be silent. She revealed a side of herself that is typically kept private: her vulnerabilities, her insecurities. Through this album, she is announcing that she will not be kept quiet and she has her own voice, according to Mabinty Quarshie for *USA TODAY*. Is Beyoncé a feminist? She allows people to determine the answer to that question for themselves.

BEYONCÉ'S FEMINIST IMAGE

Modern feminist ideas in Beyoncé's music includes those in her song "Pretty Hurts," which talks about the destructive nature of obsessing about your looks. The song "Flawless" talks about being more important than the title of "wife." There is also a quote in the song from the writer Chimamanda Ngozi Adichie that states:

> Because I am female, I am expected to aspire to marriage. I am expected to make my life choices always keeping in mind that marriage is most important. Now, marriage can be a source of joy and love and mutual support. But why do we teach girls to aspire to marriage and we don't teach boys the same? Feminist: a person who believes in the social, political, and economic equality of the sexes.

In 2014, during her Mrs. Carter Tour, the word "Feminist" appeared in big letters behind her as she sang "Flawless." She said she displayed the background during the song to give the term meaning. In an interview with *ELLE* magazine in April 2016, Beyoncé defined what feminist means to her:

ANTIFEMINIST?

In an interview with *Paper* magazine, bell hooks, a feminist writer and American scholar who examines black women and their feminist identities, said about Beyoncé and her *Lemonade* album, "Even though Beyoncé and her creative collaborators daringly offer multidimensional images of black female life, much of the album stays within a conventional stereotypical framework, where the black woman is always a victim." She has also mentioned Beyoncé before, in 2014, after seeing Beyoncé on the cover of *TIME*, stating, "I see a part of Beyoncé that is in fact, anti-feminist, that is a terrorist ... especially in terms of the impact on young girls." Is Beyoncé introducing a new aspect to the term "feminist"? She is a feminist who is proud of her body and sexuality and a woman who can make her own money in a male-dominated society.

I'm not really sure people know or understand what a feminist is, but it's very simple. It's someone who believes in equal rights for men and women. I don't understand the negative connotation of the word, or why it should exclude the opposite sex. If you are a man who believes your daughter should have the same opportunities and rights as your son, then you're a feminist.

Beyoncé hypes up the crowd during her Mrs. Carter Show World Tour, which kicked off on April 15, 2013, and ended on March 26, 2014. Every date was sold out.

In the book *Beyoncé in Formation: Remixing Black Feminism*, author Omise'eke Natasha Tinsley said about the iconic "Feminist" text displayed behind Beyoncé, "For twenty years before that performance, the words most often associated with *feminist* were *militant*, *radical*, *man-hating*. But for two days after, the word most associated with *feminist* online was Beyoncé." Tinsley also went on to discuss how the moment was also iconic because young women around the world were associating "feminist" with an African American woman.

Beyoncé attends the one-year anniversary of Chime for Change in New York City on June 3, 2014. She committed to giving the organization $500,000 to encourage projects for girls and women in the areas of education, health, and justice.

Beyoncé also works with an organization called Chime for Change. It is an organization that raises awareness about education, access to health care, and justice for women around the globe. Beyoncé is also listed as a cofounder of the organization, along with Salma Hayek.

In the September 2018 issue of *Vogue*, Beyoncé is featured as the cover story. She talked about having an emergency C-section and how she allowed herself to heal and embrace her curvier body. In her interview with *Vogue* she said, "To this day my arms, shoulders, breasts, and thighs are fuller. I have a little mommy pouch, and I'm in no rush to get rid of it. I think it's real." She also talked about loving your natural body, and that is why she made the decision to strip her hair extensions and be photographed with minimal makeup.

CHAPTER 6

JAY-Z: PHILANTHROPY, POLITICS, AND THE CRIMINAL JUSTICE SYSTEM

Shawn Carter is more than just a rap mogul and businessman. Jay-Z is an inspiration for people, especially through the Shawn Carter Foundation, which enables underprivileged young people an opportunity to go to college. He has invested his time and money into providing clean water for Africa, used his voice to urge young people to get out and vote, and also cast light on the failing criminal justice system as it pertains to African American men.

Jay-Z attends the prescreening for his documentary *Diary of Jay-Z: Water for Life* at the United Nations headquarters in New York on November 16, 2006.

THE SEARCH FOR CLEAN WATER

In 2006, Jay-Z teamed up with the United Nations (UN) to provide awareness of living conditions in Africa. There was a thirty-minute documentary entitled *Diary of Jay-Z: Water for Life.* Camera crews followed him to Angola and Durban, South Africa, where he encountered poor living conditions and lack of clean water. Jay-Z wanted to get behind a cause that affected millions of people every year. In Martin Bashir's 2006 ABC News report, Jay-Z declared, "I was looking for a cause to attach myself to. I knew I was going to some places where there was problems and as soon as I came across the problems of water, and seen the numbers that were attached to it, I was like—this is it."

> Rosa Parks sat so Martin Luther King could walk. Martin Luther King walked so Obama could run. Obama's running so we all can fly."
>
> —JAY-Z

In the UN documentary, Jay-Z met a fourteen-year-old girl named Bela and walked around with her to see what a day in her life, particularly her efforts to obtain water. She hiked a half mile (0.8 kilometer), twice each day to carry 40 pounds (18 kilograms) of water. Jay also witnessed Bela and her friends walking to school near open sewers that run down the middle of the main road. In November 2006, on the UNICEF website, Anwulika Okafor reported that Peter Gleick, president of the Pacific Institute (a research group that develops measures for water sustainability and management), said about Jay-Z's documentary, "This event is a step in the right direction. The next step would be for everyone concerned about the crisis to go out and act." Okafor noted that *Diary of Jay-Z: Water for Life* brought awareness to the public about the one billion people who lack access to clean water.

ROCK THE VOTE

In 2008, Jay-Z, P. Diddy, and Mary J. Blige introduced an "open letter to young America" to get out and register to vote because of the ongoing issues in America that needed to be addressed, according to *NME*. They declared to young voters that it was up to them to advocate for change and use their right to vote to give them a voice for the future. At the Uptown Theater in Philadelphia, Pennsylvania, Jay-Z spoke about his support for presidential candidate Barack Obama and persuaded others that it was important they cast their vote as well. Dan Martin, writing in the *Guardian* in 2008, reported that Jay-Z stood in front of the crowd and said, "Rosa Parks sat so Martin Luther King could walk. Martin Luther King walked so Obama could run. Obama's running so we all can fly."

In October 2010, Jay-Z issued a public service announcement to young voters to get out and exercise their

Jay-Z (*left*) and musician Bruce Springsteen (*far right*) show support for President Barack Obama (*center*) during a campaign appearance in Columbus, Ohio, in 2012.

right to vote. On the stage during the Bonnaroo Music Festival Jay-Z said, according to Devon Thomas for CBS News, "We absolutely changed the world—We changed the world! So it just goes to show anything is possible, fight for what's right." A volunteer group called HeadCount, a team that registers people to vote, was sent to various concerts to register attendees. Other notable musicians who used HeadCount at their concerts included John Mayer, Tom Petty, and Dave Matthews Band.

JAY-Z AND THE CRIMINAL JUSTICE SYSTEM

In 2017, Jay-Z wanted to shed light on the injustice of the American prison system. In a June 2017 article published under the name Shawn Carter in *TIME* magazine, he stated that one in nine black children have a parent who is incarcerated. He explained that the trouble was that most people arrested can't afford the bail money to get out of jail. For Father's Day 2017, Jay-Z teamed up with the organizations Southerners on New Ground and Colors of Change to bail out incarcerated men, enabling them to be with their families. Jay-Z said, "If you're from neighborhoods like the Brooklyn one I grew up in, if you're unable to afford a private attorney, then you can be disappeared into our jail system simply because you can't afford bail."

JAY-Z AND BARACK OBAMA: A FRIENDSHIP

Former president Barack Obama said that he met Jay-Z a few years into his presidency and the two hit it off and became fast friends. It was common for Jay-Z to visit the White House during the Obama administration with Beyoncé in tow, who also became good friends with First Lady Michelle Obama. On June 16, 2017, in the *Washington Post*, reporter Travis M. Andrews wrote about Jay-Z's induction into the Songwriters Hall of Fame. Jay-Z was the first hip-hop artist to receive this accolade. Barack Obama gave a prerecorded video speech in Jay-Z's honor. The former president spoke about the similarities that he and Jay-Z shared, such as growing up without a father and loving their daughters unconditionally. Obama also joked that they understand what it is like to have wives who are more popular than they are. He also mentioned, "I'm pretty sure I'm still the only president to listen to Jay-Z's music in the Oval Office. That may change at some point, but I'm pretty sure that's true now." Obama quoted Jay-Z's lyrics during his speech in Selma, Alabama, on the fiftieth anniversary of when state police officers attacked nonviolent black protesters who had fought for their right to vote in Selma, Alabama.

Beyoncé and Jay-Z attend the Justice for Trayvon rally with Trayvon's mother, Sybrina Fulton (*third from left*), and Reverend Al Sharpton (*right*) in New York City in 2013.

In March 2018, Jay-Z's Roc Nation backed a phone app to help reduce jail time. The app, called Promise, steps in during the pretrial period to help with bail money for those who cannot afford to post it. It also comes with a detailed calendar of important events, such as court dates and drug testing, as well as help with drug abuse treatment and support with housing and job training. On March 19, 2018, in *Rolling Stone*, Jay-Z stated, "Money, time and lives are wasted with the current policies. It's time for an innovative and progressive

KALIEF BROWDER

Kalief Browder, a sixteen-year-old from the Bronx, was arrested for stealing a backpack. He was not able to make bail because his family didn't have the money and he was also being held on a prior offense. He was sent to Rikers Island in New York to await his trial, which was later dismissed, but he spent eight hundred days in solitary confinement. At the age of twenty-two, he took his own life because of severe post-traumatic stress disorder (PTSD). His story touched Jay-Z, and he started to focus his attention on the inequalities in the American prison system. Jay-Z was the executive producer for a documentary based on Browder's life, *Time: The Kalief Browder Story*. In an article in *Rolling Stone* on March 9, 2017, Jay-Z said, "There's got to be an awakening across the country. It doesn't have to be looking at the White House or senators. I think it's about looking at what's happening in your county, your town, your city, right now. If Americans can think small, they can do much bigger things."

technology that offers sustainable solutions to tough problems." Jay-Z has focused his attention on the failing criminal justice system in the wake of the death of Kalief Browder.

Sean Combs & Shawn Carter — 100

DATE September 9, 2005

PAY TO THE ORDER OF The American Red Cross $ 1,000,000.00

One Million Dollars

DOLLARS

MEMO Hurricane Katrina Relief — Sean Combs Shawn Carter

⑊000110203⑊ 71021 48265⑊ 2284

In September 2005, Jay-Z, pictured with fellow rapper and businessman Sean "P. Diddy" Combs, donated $1 million to the American Red Cross to aid in Hurricane Katrina relief.

Jay-Z is an eminent celebrity who uses his voice and power to shine light on important issues. As noted on Look to the Stars, a website that showcases how celebrities are giving back, Jay was involved with twelve charity organizations and has supported more than fifteen causes, including AIDS and HIV, disaster relief, cancer, and disadvantaged youth. According to August Brown of the *Los Angeles Times*, during an interview with Elliott Wilson of Rap Radar, Jay-Z remarked, "My presence is charity."

CHAPTER 7

THE CARTERS

The Carters—Beyoncé and Jay-Z—have established themselves as a billion-dollar power couple. Beyoncé attributes her wealth to her hard work and Jay-Z has a lot of money tied into his lucrative businesses, such as TIDAL, the music-streaming service. Needless to say, there is no limit to the heights of where this power duo can go and what they can accomplish alone and together.

A JOINT VIDEO

In 2018, Beyoncé and Jay-Z debuted their song "Apes**t" off their new joint album *Everything Is Love*. The joint video opens with the power couple

The Raft of Medusa by Théodore Géricault (ca. 1819) is a painting that depicts the aftermath of a shipwreck. In 2018, Jay-Z rapped in front of the painting, which is housed in the Louvre Museum in Paris, while making the joint music video with Beyoncé.

wearing pastel suits in front of Leonardo da Vinci's painting the *Mona Lisa* (ca. 1503–19), which is housed in the Louvre Museum in Paris, France. The *Mona Lisa* is one of the most famous paintings in history. As the camera pans out, the focus isn't on the *Mona Lisa* but on Jay-Z and Beyoncé. *They* are the art that is the focus in the music video. The album was a surprise release in June 2018, and as of November 2018, the video has more than 135 million views on YouTube.

The video shows Jay-Z rapping in front of Théodore Géricault's painting *The Raft of Medusa* (ca. 1819) and signifies the end of the tumultuous times for Bey and Jay in their marriage, according to Khal for *Complex*. The background of the story depicted in the painting is one of tragedy and triumph. A French boat sets sail to colonize Senegal, but the captain wasn't very experienced and the boat crashed on a sandbar. The boat lacked enough lifeboats to save the entire crew so 150 men were left behind to build a raft. Only ten men survived, and the painting captures the moment that a rescue vessel is spotted on the horizon, which signifies hope for the crew.

Then Beyoncé gets into formation in front of Jacques-Louis David's painting *The Consecration of the Emperor Napoleon I and the Crowning of Empress Joséphine in Notre-Dame Cathedral on December 2, 1804* (1806–07). She parallels herself with Empress Joséphine in a statement in which she said she has crowned herself queen and doesn't need the establishment to confirm that she is queen. The background of this painting is that Napoleon crowned himself emperor, without having the pope officially consecrate him as emperor. In the painting, Napoleon, in turn, crowns the empress. According to an article in *TIME* magazine on June 19, 2018, art historian Alexandra Thomas said, "It appears that Queen Bey is not looking to the establishment for confirmation of her greatness."

Another notable piece of art in the video is the Greek sculpture *Aphrodite*, also known as the Venus de Milo (ca. 100 BCE). The camera shows Beyoncé moving her body to match the "S curve" of the pose in the statue in a statement about what constitutes beauty. The Venus de Milo showcases classical standards of beauty, and Beyoncé posing in front of the statue symbolizes her power to play on the idea of standardized beauty. Thomas said, "For Beyoncé to have these black performers with her and her husband, performing in front of an iconic piece of ancient Greek sculpture—which probably symbolizes European beauty standards more than anything—was really powerful."

THE LOUVRE AND THE APES**T TOUR

The music video was released on June 16, 2018, and soon after, the Louvre Museum began offering a ninety-minute tour of all the artwork represented in the "Apes**t" music video. The tour is self-guided, and it doesn't give the historical context behind the artwork but instead shows people the parts of the museum where the music video was filmed. It is called the Jay-Z et Beyoncé au Louvre tour. It enables the visitor to determine for himself or herself why the power couple might have chosen to represent the specific pieces of art in the music video. The Louvre, no doubt, is cashing in on the success of the music video and the power couple behind it.

EVERYTHING IS LOVE

After the releases of Beyoncé's *Lemonade* and Jay-Z's *4:44*, the couple released *Everything Is Love* without an announcement on TIDAL. Beyoncé and Jay-Z are no strangers to releasing albums without an announcement. This album represents a reconciliation

> [Beyoncé is] my soul mate, the person I love … For us, we chose to fight for our love. For our family."
> —JAY-Z

of their relationship and a hope for the future. It imparts the love they share between them after the years of Jay-Z's adultery accusations. The album is a sort of rebirth of them as a power couple. Beyoncé released *Lemonade* in 2016 and Jay-Z released *4:44* in 2017, both on TIDAL and both without any of their fans knowing beforehand about the releases.

The third installment, and conclusion, to their relationship story, *Everything Is Love*, brings everything about their union into context and showcases a happily ever after ending for the couple. In an interview on the premiere of the *Van Jones Show* on CNN in January 2018, Van Jones asked Jay-Z why he decided to fight for his marriage. Jay-Z said that his wife was "my soul mate, the person I love … For us, we chose to fight for our love. For our family. To give our kids a different outcome. To break that cycle for black men and women." *Everything Is Love* came after the couple renewed

Beyoncé accepts the Grammy Award for Best Urban Contemporary Album, for *Lemonade*, on February 12, 2017.

their vows in April 2018 for their ten-year wedding anniversary. Fans had speculated that the Carters might have renewed their vows because of the home videos that were shown on big screens during the On the Run II Tour that started on June 6, 2018, in Cardiff, Wales. In one home video, Beyoncé and Jay-Z are seen bowing their heads in an intimate ceremony surrounded by their children. They were both adorned in white. Beyoncé announced on her website on September 6, 2018, a couple of days after her thirty-seventh birthday, that she and Jay-Z renewed their wedding vows on their ten-year anniversary. In an article in *US Weekly* on September 6, 2018, Beyoncé recapped, "At 36, I became a new mother of three. I breastfed my twins. I renewed my vows with my husband of 10 years. My husband and I released our album together, *Everything Is Love*. And we've been touring

with our family around the world, and loving it. This year has been monumental for me."

Jay-Z pumps up the crowd on his 4:44 Tour at the Barclays Center in Brooklyn in New York City. His tour went to twenty-nine locations in North America in 2017.

ON THE RUN II

On June 6, 2018, the Carters kicked off their On the Run II Tour in Cardiff, Wales, and wrapped it up on October 2, 2018, in Vancouver, British Columbia. On the Run II showcased a new side of the couple, one in which Jay-Z stayed more in the background while Beyoncé was front and center, suggesting a shift in power. In an article in the *New York Times*,

Jon Caramanica says about the concert, "What has changed is that, in that time, Beyoncé has become the pre-eminent performer in pop, and the public power dynamic of their relationship has switched—she is the world beater now, and he is in the background." Toward the end of the concert, Jay-Z started with his song "U Don't Know," and a screen behind him showed a group of all-female horn players. This action was obviously a very "Beyoncé" move and showed that he is learning from his wife and

Beyoncé and Jay-Z kick off their On the Run II Tour in Cardiff, Wales, imbuing happiness as the power couple perform before their fans.

making his art better, while his partner, Beyoncé, stands beside him.

Mark Sutherland wrote a review of the first show of On the Run II in *Rolling Stone,* praising it, and commenting, "But in spite of a pair of albums—Beyoncé's betrayal opus *Lemonade* and Jay-Z's confessional *4:44*—that shed light on the truth behind those seemingly perfect lifestyles, On the Run II ultimately seemed to focus more on the fairytale than the harsh reality." Displayed on big screens behind the couple during the concert was the text "This. Is. Real. Love." The concert and tour On the Run II showed a united Jay and Bey, an unstoppable force, even if the overall context of the show seemed exaggerated. The question remains, though, is this the real couple or is this couple a fantasy?

WHAT'S NEXT FOR THESE SUPERSTARS?

The future looks bright for the billion-dollar mega superstars. In 2018, they officially became a billion-dollar power couple, and their family expanded as well. They welcomed twins, Sir and Rumi Carter, on June 13, 2017. The couple's jubilant On the Run II Tour wrapped up in October 2018, a tour that successfully earned the Carters $5 million each night. Jay-Z's business ventures are lucrative and will continue to be a good source of income for the couple for years to come. Beyoncé keeps on dominating the music industry and works on her multimillion-dollar endorsement deals.

The power couple's single "Apes**t" showed the world how much swagger they have by renting out the Louvre Museum to film the music video. The song itself expresses the financial successes they share. Jay-Z raps about a motorcade bringing Blue Ivy to school. Beyoncé sings about designer fabrics and expensive luxuries she can afford, such as Lamborghinis, private jets, and expensive jewelry. The music video itself signifies that they are as impressionable as the art shown in the video. The video almost disregards the famous artwork represented within it. Instead it forces

A RICH POWER COUPLE

Beyoncé and Jay-Z have been named one of the richest power couples in the world according to Business Insider in March 2018. In 2018, the couple surpassed the billion-dollar mark and were worth an estimated $1.2 billion. It was reported that the couple gifted their daughter Blue Ivy a diamond-encrusted Barbie doll for her first birthday that was valued at roughly $80,000. They own a $40-million private jet and a $4-million private island in the Bahamas, and they regularly vacation in Paris, France, at the Hotel Le Meurice, renting a penthouse for $20,000 per night. These examples are just some of the luxuries this billionaire couple can enjoy!

the viewer to focus all attention on Beyoncé, Jay-Z, and their dancers, almost declaring that the art they create together will leave as significant an imprint on the world as the *Mona Lisa* and other classic art pieces have. At the end of the music video, Beyoncé and Jay-Z turn to look at the *Mona Lisa*. As reported by Cady Lang in *TIME*, Kimberly Drew, an art curator and social media editor for the Metropolitan Museum of Art in New York, said, "The Carters are exercising as both consumers and creators of art."

Beyoncé and Jay-Z, music royalty and considered the most powerful couple in the entertainment industry by most reviewers, have dominated music, entertainment, and business for more than a decade. Both are inspirational in their own right because they started with a dream, and with hard work and determination they each rose to success. With their chart-topping singles, Grammy wins, multimillion-dollar companies and endorsements, and millions of record sales, Beyoncé and Jay-Z show no sign of relinquishing their place at the top. What the future holds for this power couple is one that is bright and littered with dollar bills!

1969 Shawn Corey Carter, later known as Jay-Z, is born on December 4 in Brooklyn, New York.

1981 Beyoncé Giselle Knowles is born on September 4 in Houston, Texas.

1992 Girl's Tyme tape their appearance on *Star Search* in November.

1996 Jay-Z releases *Reasonable Doubt*, his first album.

1998 Destiny's Child releases their first single off of their album, *Destiny's Child*, titled "No, No, No." Jay-Z releases *Vol. 2... Hard Knock Life*.

1999 Destiny's Child releases their second album, *The Writing's on the Wall*. Jay-Z releases *Vol. 3... Life and Times of S. Carter*. Jay-Z stabs producer Lance Rivera at the Kit Kat Club.

2001 Jay-Z releases his album *Blueprint*. Destiny's Child releases their third album, *Survivor*.

2002 Beyoncé and Jay-Z meet and collaborate on their first song, "'03 Bonnie and Clyde."

2003 Beyoncé releases her first solo album, *Dangerously in Love*, and her hit "Crazy in Love" rises to number one on *Billboard's* charts. Jay-Z releases *The Black Album*.

His farewell concert was held at Madison Square Garden on November 25.

2006 Beyoncé releases her second solo album, *B'Day*.

2008 Beyoncé releases *I Am...Sasha Fierce*. Beyoncé and Jay-Z marry in a private ceremony in New York City.

2011 Beyoncé releases her fourth solo album, *4*. Beyoncé announces she is pregnant at the MTV Music Awards.

2012 Blue Ivy Carter is born on January 7 in New York City.

2014 Beyoncé releases her fifth solo album, *Beyoncé*. Beyoncé and Jay-Z headline a tour, On the Run.

2016 Beyoncé releases *Lemonade*, which draws speculation about Jay-Z's infidelity.

2017 Jay-Z releases *4:44* on TIDAL. Sir and Rumi Carter are born on June 13.

2018 Beyoncé and Jay-Z debut their song "Apes**t" off their new joint album, *Everything Is Love*. In June, the Louvre Museum offers a ninety-minute tour of all the artwork represented in the "Apes**t" music video. Beyoncé and Jay-Z headline the On the Run II Tour.

accredited Describing an organization or person that is authorized with all of the essential requirements.

album A collection of musical pieces by a recording artist that is made available for the consumer on a CD, through online streaming, or on a vinyl record.

alter ego A secondary identity that a person adopts.

American Music Awards (AMAs) An award program that celebrates the current music scene. Unlike the Grammy Awards, the AMAs are determined by the public and fans.

Billboard chart A chart that tabulates the popularity of a song or an album on a weekly basis.

bootleg An item that is made and sold illegally.

catalyze To bring about or cause a change.

chief executive officer (CEO) An individual who makes business decisions and is head of an organization.

consecrate To make or declare sacred.

conspiracy theory A theory that describes an event, or series of events, derived from a secret plot by prominent figures.

discriminate To treat people unjustly because they belong to a certain group, such as a race, religion, or gender.

Grammy An annual award given out to outstanding musicians in various categories by the National Academy of Recording Arts and Sciences.

Guinness World Records An annual publication that focuses on record-breaking accomplishments.

post-traumatic stress disorder (PTSD) A serious disorder that can develop when a person has been exposed to a mentally or emotionally traumatic event.

prejudice A preconceived judgment about a person or thing not based on actual experience or facts.

Rally 4 Peace A benefit concert in Baltimore, Maryland, on May 10, 2015, headlined by performing artist Prince after the Baltimore protests.

rap A style of music that incorporates rhyme to a beat.

record label A company that works with artists to produce their music and sell their records.

rhythm and blues (R&B) A popular genre of music that incorporates funk, soul, hip-hop, and blues.

segregation The practice of keeping people separate or isolated, generally those of different classes, races, genders, or religions.

surrogate A woman who carries the child of another woman, usually because of infertility.

Video Music Awards (VMAs) Awards that honor the best music videos by the popular cable channel MTV.

Answer the Call
New York Police & Fire Widows' & Children's
     Benefit Fund
156 West 56th Street, Suite 901
New York, NY 10019
(646) 731-9630
Website: http://www.answerthecall.org
Facebook and Instagram: @AnswerTheCallNYC
Twitter: @answerthecall
Following the death of a first responder, Answer
     the Call provides that first responder's family
     with $25,000 to help with the burden of their
     loss. Answer the Call also assists the widow or
     widower with an annual stipend.

BeyGood Houston
Bread of Life, Inc.
2019 Crawford Street
Houston, TX 77002
(713) 659-3237
Website: https://www.beyonce.com
     /beygoodhouston
Twitter: @BeyGood
Facebook: @beygood
BeyGood Houston is a part of BeyGood. Its
     mission is to help rebuild the city of Houston
     after the devastation of Hurricane Harvey.
     BeyGood Houston assists families that were
     displaced by the hurricane by providing shelter
     and temporary housing.

Chime for Change
Website: http://www.chimeforchange.org
Facebook, Instagram, and Twitter:
     @ChimeForChange
Chime for Change is an organization that raises
     awareness about education, access to health
     care, and justice for women around the globe.

HeadCount
104 West 29th Street
New York, NY 10001
(866) Our-Vote
Website: https://www.headcount.org
Facebook, Instagram, and Twitter:
     @HeadCountOrg
HeadCount is a street team that is sent out to
     concerts to encourage young people to register
     to vote. HeadCount has registered more than
     five hundred thousand voters since 2004.

Prince's Trust
Website: https://www.princes-trust.org.uk
Instagram and Twitter: @PrincesTrust
Facebook: @princestrust
The Prince's Trust helps people ages eleven to
     thirty who are struggling to find a job or having
     challenges in school. Many of the people it
     assists are (or have been) homeless, have
     mental health issues, have been arrested, or
     are facing jail time.

Shawn Carter Foundation
Website: https://www.shawncartersf.com
Instagram and Twitter: @ShawnCarterSF
Facebook: @SCScholarship
The Shawn Carter Foundation provides money
    for scholarships for disadvantaged youths.
    The foundation raises money for college
    scholarships, college-counseling programs,
    study-abroad opportunities, college visits, and
    personal development.

Songwriters Hall of Fame
330 West 58th Street, Suite 411
New York, NY 10019
(212) 957-9230
Website: https://www.songhall.org
Twitter: @SongwritersHOF
Facebook: @songhall
The Songwriters Hall of Fame recognizes and
    celebrates great songwriters. A person can
    qualify for induction into the Songwriters Hall of
    Fame twenty years after the release of a song.
    Jay-Z was inducted in 2017.

Associated Press. *Beyoncé: From Destiny's Child to Independent Woman*. Miami, FL: Mango Media, Inc., 2015.

Beaumont, Mark. *Jay-Z: The King of America*. London, UK: Omnibus Press, 2012.

Burlingame, Jeff. *Jay-Z: A Biography of a Hip-Hop Icon* (African-American Icons). Berkeley Heights, NJ: Enslow Publishers, Inc., 2014.

Dann, Sarah. *Beyoncé* (Superstars!). New York, NY: Crabtree Publishing, 2014.

Forte, Virginia, ed. *The 100 Most Influential Entertainers of Stage and Screen* (The Britannica Guide to the World's Most Influential People). New York, NY: Britannica Educational Publishing, 2015.

Gordon, Stephen. *Jay-Z CEO of Hip-Hop*. Minneapolis, MN: Lerner Publishing Group, Inc., 2013.

Greenburg, Zack O'Malley. *Empire State of Mind: How Jay Z Went From Street Corner to Corner Office*. Rev. Paperback ed. New York, NY: Portfolio/Penguin Books, 2015.

Hill, Z. B. *Beyoncé* (Superstars of Hip-Hop). Broomall, PA: Mason Crest Publishing, 2013.

Kampff, Joseph. *Jay Z: Rapper and Businessman* (Exceptional African Americans). New York, NY: Enslow Publishing, 2016.

Lajiness, Katie. *Beyoncé* (Big Buddy Pop Biographies). Minneapolis, MN: ABDO Publishing, 2017.

Oswald, Vanessa. *Jay-Z: Building a Hip-Hop Empire* (People in the News). New York, NY: Lucent Press, 2019.

Pointer, Anna. *Beyoncé: Running the World: The Biography*. London, UK: Coronet, 2014.

Schwartz, Heather. *Beyoncé: The Queen of Pop*. Minneapolis, MN: Lerner Publications, 2018.

Susienka, Alexander. *Beyoncé* (Celebrity Entrepreneurs). New York, NY: Cavendish Square, 2015.

Taraborrelli, J. Randy. *Becoming Beyoncé: The Untold Story*. New York, NY: Grand Central Publishing, 2016.

Tinsley, Omise'eke Natasha. *Beyoncé in Formation: Remixing Black Feminism*. Austin, TX: University of Texas Press, 2018.

Ahmed, Insanul, and Brendan Frederick, Dave Bry, David Drake, Donnie Kwak, Max Goldberg, Noah Callahan-Bever, Ross Scarano, and Frazier Tharpe. "Ranking Jay-Z's Albums from Worst to Best." *Complex*, September 11, 2018. https://www.complex.com/music/2018/09 /ranking-jay-zs-albums-from-worst-to-best.

Andrews, Travis. "Obama Describes His Bond with Jay Z." *Washington Post*, June 16, 2017. https://www.washingtonpost.com /news/morning-mix/wp/2017/06/16/obama -describes-his-bond-to-jay-z/?utm_term =.0f78836071fb.

Bashir, Martin. "Jay-Z's Battle for Clean Water." ABC News, November 27, 2006. https:// abcnews.go.com/Nightline/story?id=2681905 &page=1.

Beaumont, Mark. *Jay-Z: The King of America*. London, UK: Omnibus Press, 2012.

Billboard staff. "Beyoncé Passes Madonna with the Most VMAs Ever." *Billboard*, August 29, 2016. https://www.billboard.com/articles/events/vma /7487949/beyonce-most-vmas-madonna.

Billboard staff. "Ex-Destiny's Child Members Sue Over '*Survivor*.'" *Billboard*, February 28, 2002. https://www.billboard.com/articles /news/76633/ex-destinys-child-members-sue -over-survivor.

Brown, August. "Jay Z on Social Responsibility: 'My Presence Is Charity.'" *Los Angeles Times*, July

26, 2013. http://articles.latimes.com/2013/
jul/26/entertainment/la-et-ms-jay-z-on
-social-responsibility-my-presence-is-charity
-20130726.

Burlingame, Jeff. *Jay-Z: A Biography of a Hip-Hop Icon* (African-American Icons). Berkeley Heights, NJ: Enslow Publishers, Inc., 2014.

Caramanica, Jon. "Beyoncé and Jay-Z Squeeze Triumph From Reconciliation." *New York Times*, August 3, 2018. https://www.nytimes.com /2018/08/03/arts/music/beyonce-jay-z-on -the-run-ii-tour-review.html.

Carter, Shawn. "Jay-Z: For Father's Day, I'm Taking On the Exploitative Bail Industry." *TIME*, June 16, 2017. http://time.com/4821547/jay -z-racism-bail-bonds.

Caulfield, Keith. "Jay-Z by the Numbers: From 1996 Chart Debut to Record-Extending No. 1 Album '4:44.'" *Billboard*, July 17, 2017. https://www.billboard.com/articles/columns /chart-beat/7866305/jay-z-by-the-numbers -billboard-charts.

Clarke, Stewart. "Jay-Z's Rock Nation Joins BBC's 'Noughts & Crosses' Series." *Variety*, October 4, 2018. https://variety.com/2018/tv/news /jay-z-roc-nation-bbc-noughts-and-crosses -series-1202968427.

Dockterman, Eliana. "Flawless: 5 Lessons in Modern Feminism From Beyoncé." *TIME*, December 17, 2013. http://time.com/1851

/flawless-5-lessons-in-modern-feminism-from
-beyonce.

Forte, Virginia, ed. *The 100 Most Influential
Entertainers of Stage and Screen* (The
Britannica Guide to the World's Most Influential
People). New York, NY: Britannica Educational
Publishing, 2015.

George, Rachel. "Ariana Grande, Beyonce &
More Among DoSomething.org's List of Most
Charitable Celebrities of 2017." *Billboard*,
December 27, 2017. https://www.billboard
.com/articles/news/lifestyle/8085001
/dosomething-most-charitable-celebs-list
-chance-the-rapper.

Gottesman, Tamar. "EXCLUSIVE: Beyoncé Wants
to Change the Conversation." *ELLE*, April 4,
2016. https://www.elle.com/fashion/a35286
/beyonce-elle-cover-photos.

Greenburg, Zack O'Malley. "Beyoncé and Jay Z
Are Officially a Billion-Dollar Couple." *Forbes*,
May 17, 2017. https://www.forbes.com/sites
/zackomalleygreenburg/2017/05/17/beyonce
-and-jay-z-are-officially-a-billion-dollar
-couple/#1e3f2e37478e.

Greenburg, Zack O'Malley. *Empire State of Mind:
How Jay Z Went From Street Corner to Corner
Office*. Rev. Paperback ed. New York, NY:
Portfolio/Penguin Books, 2015.

Greenburg, Zack O'Malley. "The Forbes Five: Hip-
Hop's Wealthiest Artists, 2018." *Forbes*, March

1, 2018. https://www.forbes.com/sites
/zackomalleygreenburg/2018/03/01/the
-forbes-five-hip-hops-wealthiest-artists
-2018/#56e0eef147c1.

Greenburg, Zack O'Malley. "Jay-Z and Beyoncé
Are Now Worth a Combined $1.255 Billion—
and Counting." *Forbes*, July 12, 2018. https://
www.forbes.com/sites
/zackomalleygreenburg/2018/07/12/jay-z
-and-beyonce-are-now-worth-a-combined-1
-255-billion-and-counting/#5d3b384a1ec6.

Hautman, Nicholas. "Beyoncé Confirms She and
Jay-Z Renewed Their Vows in Honor of 10th
Wedding Anniversary." *US Weekly*, September
6, 2018. https://www.usmagazine.com
/celebrity-news/news/beyonce-confirms-she
-and-jay-z-renewed-their-wedding-vows.

Hill, Z. B. *Beyoncé* (Superstars of Hip-Hop).
Broomall, PA: Mason Crest Publishing, 2013.

Hobson, Janell. "Beyoncé's Fierce Feminism." *Ms.*
magazine, March 7, 2015. http://msmagazine
.com/blog/2015/03/07/beyonces-fierce
-feminism.

Hoffower, Hillary. "Here's How Much Money 19
Rich and Famous Power Couples Are Worth."
Business Insider, September 4, 2018. https://
www.businessinsider.com/famous-rich-power
-couples-net-worth-2018-8.

Jefferson, J'na. "Beyoncé and Jay-Z 'Apesh*t'
Video Inspires Tour at the Louvre." *Vibe*, July 6,

2018. https://www.vibe.com/2018/07/beyonce
-jay-z-the-louvre-tour.

Jefferson, J'na. "Jay-Z's 40/40 Club Hosting
Exclusive Hurricane Relief Event." *Vibe*, October
4, 2017. https://www.vibe.com/2017/10/jay-z
-hurricane-relief-event.

Kampff, Joseph. *Jay Z: Rapper and Businessman*
(Exceptional African Americans). New York, NY:
Enslow Publishing, 2016.

Keaney, Quinn. "Beyoncé Schools Everyone
on Body Image and Feminism in Her Latest
Surprise Video." MTV, December 12, 2014.
http://www.mtv.com/news/2024545/beyonce
-yours-mine-video-feminism.

Khal, and Steven Chew. "Breaking Down the
Hidden Meaning in Beyoncé and Jay-Z's
Apesh*t Video." *Complex*, June 19, 2018.
https://www.complex.com/music/2018/06
/breaking-down-hidden-meaning-in-beyonce
-jay-z-apesht-video.

King, Alexandra. "Jay-Z on Mending His Marriage
to Beyoncé: We Chose to "Break That Cycle."
CNN, Updated January 28, 2018. https://
www.cnn.com/2018/01/27/us/jay-z-on
-marriage-cnntv/index.html.

Lang, Cady. "Art History Experts Explain the
Meaning of the Art in Beyoncé and Jay Z's
'Apesh-t' Video." *TIME*, June 19, 2018. http://
time.com/5315275/art-references-meaning
-beyonce-jay-z-apeshit-louvre-music-video.

Leight, Elias. "Jay Z, Harvey Weinstein, Talk Kalief Browder Doc at New York Event." *Rolling Stone*, March 9, 2017. https://www.rollingstone.com /music/music-news/jay-z-harvey-weinstein-talk -kalief-browder-doc-at-new-york-event -107809.

Lewis, Taylor. "The 10 Not-So-Publicized Times Jay Z And Beyonce Gave Back." *Essence*, February 1, 2017. https://www.essence.com/celebrity /black-celeb-couples/10-not-so-publicized -times-jay-z-and-beyonce-gave-back.

Lipsky-Karasz, Elisa. "Beyoncé's Baby Love." *Harper's Bazaar*, October 11, 2011. https:// www.harpersbazaar.com/celebrity/latest/news /a825/beyonces-baby-love-interview-1111.

Macatee, Rebecca. "Inside Beyoncé and Jay-Z's Billion Dollar Empire." E! News, September 4, 2018. https://www.eonline.com/news/964455 /inside-beyonce-and-jay-z-s-billion-dollar -empire.

Martin, Dan. "Jay-Z: Obama's Running So We Can All Fly." *Guardian*, November 5, 2008. https://www.theguardian.com/music/2008 /nov/05/jayz-falloutboy.

Mitchell, Gail. "Shawn Carter Foundation and eBay for Charity Partner for College Campaign." *Billboard*, May 15, 2017. https:// www.billboard.com/articles/business /7793127/shawn-carter-foundation-ebay -for-charity-college-campaign-auction.

Montgomery, Sarah Jasmine. "Jay-Z Addresses

Secret Son Rumors on 'Heard About Us.'"
Complex, June 17, 2018. https://www
.complex.com/music/2018/06/jay-z
-addresses-secret-son-rumor-on-heard
-about-us.

Nilles, Billy. "*Destiny's Child* Turns 20: A Look at
the Humble Beginnings of Beyoncé's Game-
Changing Career." E! News, February 17,
2018. https://www.eonline.com/news/914552
/destiny-s-child-turns-20-a-look-back-at-the
-humble-beginnings-of-beyonce-s-game
-changing-career.

NME. "P Diddy, Jay-Z Urge 'Young America' To
Vote." NME, October 6, 2008. https://www
.nme.com/news/music/p-diddy-44-1333129.

Ocbazghi, Emmanuel, and Alana Yzola. "The
Hidden Meanings behind Beyoncé and Jay-Z's
'APES---' Video." Business Insider, June 19,
2018. https://www.businessinsider.com/hidden
-meanings-beyonce-jay-z-ape-video-napoleon
-louvre-museum-2018-6.

Okafer, Anwulika. "Jay-Z Presents 'Water for
Life'—A Video Call to Action on the Global
Water Crisis." UNICEF, November 17, 2006.
https://www.unicef.org/wash/3942_36634
.html.

Oswald, Vanessa. *Jay-Z: Building a Hip-Hop
Empire* (People in the News). New York, NY:
Lucent Press, 2019.

People staff. "Beyoncé and Jay-Z: Power Couple."
People, April 5, 2005. https://people.com

/celebrity/beyonc-jay-z-power-couple/#playing
-coy.

Quarshie, Mabinty. "Beyoncé's 'Lemonade' Album
but a Sip of Her Evolving Feminist Story." *USA
TODAY*, February 20, 2017.https://www
.usatoday.com/story/life/nation-now/2017
/02/20/beyoncs-lemonade-album-but-sip
-her-evolving-feminist-story/96472706.

Ramirez, Erika. "Beyoncé's '4:' Track-by-Track
Review." *Billboard*, June 28, 2011. https://
www.billboard.com/articles/news/469592
/beyonces-4-track-by-track-review.

Recording Academy Grammy Awards. "Artist:
Beyoncé." Grammy.com. Retrieved September
19, 2018. https://www.grammy.com/grammys/
artists/beyonc%C3%A9-knowles.

Recording Academy Grammy Awards. "Artist:
Jay-Z." Grammy.com. Retrieved September
19, 2018. https://www.grammy.com
/grammys/artists/jay-z.

Reliable Source, The. "Jay-Z's Charity: A Closer
Look at the Shawn Carter Foundation."
Washington Post, November 19, 2013. https://
www.washingtonpost.com/news
/reliable-source/wp/2013/11/19/jay-zs
-charity-a-closer-look-at-the-shawn-carter
-foundation/?utm_term=.8ea60646ab8d.

Rolling Stone. "Jay-Z's Roc Nation Supports App to
Improve Criminal Justice System." March 19,
2018. https://www.rollingstone.com/music

/music-news/jay-zs-roc-nation-supports-app -to-improve-criminal-justice-system-2-253626.

Rose, Lacey. "Inside Beyoncé's Entertainment Empire." *Forbes*, June 4, 2009. https://www .forbes.com/forbes/2009/0622/celebrity-09 -jay-z-sasha-fierce-inside-beyonce-empire .html#30e79c172f68.

Schwartz, Heather. *Beyoncé: The Queen of Pop*. Minneapolis, MN: Lerner Publications, 2018.

Simmons, Ken. "Beyoncé & Jay-Z Offering Free 'On The Run II' Tickets for Acts of Kindness." *Good Morning America*, June 5, 2018. https:// www.goodmorningamerica.com/culture/story /beyonc-jay-offering-free-run-ii-tickets-acts -55656227.

Smee, Sebastian. "Stunting on the Louvre: Beyoncé and Jay-Z and the Art of Swagger." *Washington Post*, June 19, 2018. https://www .washingtonpost.com/entertainment/museums /stunting-on-the-louvre-beyonce-jay-z-and-the -art-of-swagger/2018/06/19/bc48dae0-73cd -11e8-b4b7-308400242c2e_story.html?utm _term=.b4b5bd1d6db7.

Song, Sandra. "bell hooks Critiques Beyoncé's Depictions of Feminism and Race in 'Lemonade.'" *Paper*, May 10, 2016. http:// www.papermag.com/beyonce-bell-hooks -lemonade-1789047140.html.

Sonny, Julian. "How Jay Z and Dame Dash Went from Business Partners to Sworn Enemies." Elite

Daily, March 17, 2015. https://www.elitedaily
.com/music/jay-z-dame-dash-business
-partners-sworn-enemies/968151.

Sutherland, Mark. "Beyoncé, Jay-Z Stand United at
Epic 'On the Run II' Tour Kickoff." *Rolling Stone*,
June 7, 2018. https://www.rollingstone
.com/music/music-live-reviews/beyonce-jay-z
-stand-united-at-epic-on-the-run-ii-tour
-kickoff-629550.

Taraborrelli, J. Randy. *Becoming Beyoncé: The
Untold Story*. New York, NY: Grand Central
Publishing, 2016.

Thomas, Devon. "Jay-Z Encourages Youth to "Vote
Again" in TV Ad for HeadCount." CBS News,
October 13, 2010. https://www.cbsnews.com
/news/jay-z-encourages-youth-to-vote-again
-in-tv-ad-for-headcount.

Tinsley, Omise'eke Natasha. *Beyoncé in
Formation: Remixing Black Feminism*. Austin,
TX: University of Texas Press, 2018.

US Weekly Staff. "Jay-Z: I Shot My Brother When
I Was 12." *US Weekly*, November 22, 2010.
https://www.usmagazine.com/entertainment
/news/jay-z-i-shot-my-brother-when-i-was
-12-20102211.

Vogue Staff. "Beyoncé in Her Own Words: Her
Life, Her Body, Her Heritage." *Vogue*, August 6,
2018. https://www.vogue.com/article/beyonce
-september-issue-2018.

Wallace, Amy. "Miss Millennium: Beyoncé." *GQ*, January 10, 2013. https://www.gq.com /story/beyonce-cover-story-interview-gq -february-2013.

Wegner, Yvonne, and Wesley Case. "Thousands Turn Out for Prince's 'Rally 4 Peace' Benefit Concert." *Baltimore Sun*, May 10, 2015. http:// www.baltimoresun.com/entertainment/music /bs-md-prince-concert-20150510-story.html.

"Crazy in Love," 20–21, 32

D

Dangerously in Love, 20, 32
Dash, Damon, 27, 34
Davis, Ashley, 12, 14
Def Jam Records, 30, 34
Destiny's Child, 14, 15–19, 60
  Grammy Awards, 17
  lawsuit against Mathew Knowles, 17–18
Destiny's Child album, 15
Diary of Jay-Z: Water for Life, 69–70

E

Everything Is Love, 33, 77, 81

F

Formation Scholars, 57
Formation World Tour, 6
40/40 Club, 34, 52, 54
4 album, 41
4:44, 46, 81, 85
Franklin, Farrah, 17, 18

G

Girl's Tyme, 8, 12, 14

Global Citizen, 54
Grammy Awards, 8, 17, 19, 20, 22, 29, 33, 46
Gray, Freddie, 55

H

HeadCount, 72
Headliners Hair Salon, 10, 14–15
Hurricane Harvey, 52
Hurricane Katrina, 51
Hurricane Maria, 52–53

I

I Am . . . Sasha Fierce, 22
In My Lifetime ... Vol. 1, 27, 29
Ivy Park gym-wear line, 7

J

Jay-Z
  adultery accusations, 46, 47, 81
  albums and awards count, 8
  birth, 23
  and brother's shooting, 26–27
  childhood, 23, 25, 26
  and clean drinking water, 69–70

ABOUT THE AUTHOR

Jacqueline Parrish has a bachelor of arts degree in English literature from Appalachian State University. While attending college, she wrote for a local publication. Parrish enjoys reading, book collecting, and barre class. She has been a fan of Beyoncé and Jay-Z's since the beginning of their musical careers. She currently resides in Kalamazoo, Michigan, with her daughter, Madeline.

PHOTO CREDITS